Bert Wigg AMAZING Ears

David Cox and Erica James

Illustrated by Pat McCarthy

OXFORD
UNIVERSITY PRESS

As clever as Prince Cecil

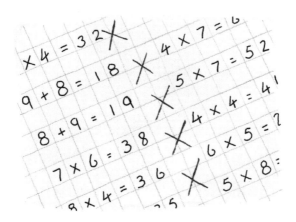

'Five times five!' said Mrs Lines.

She had a way of saying things softly
that sounded as if she was shouting
at you.

Everyone in the class wrote something
down, except Bertie.

Bertie chewed on the end of his pencil.
What was the answer? He wished he
could work it out. But he couldn't.

The trouble was, Bertie was no good at sums. No matter how hard he tried, he couldn't remember past his three times table.

He felt his ears beginning to twitch again.

Sadie Smith looked at Bertie and started to smile.

Mrs Lines looked up and said, sharply, 'Sadie! What is the matter?'

Sadie blushed. 'Nothing, Mrs Lines,' she said. But Mrs Lines could see for herself that Bertie's ears were wiggling. The trouble was, Bertie's ears didn't wiggle just a little bit. They wiggled and waggled as if they were waving at you.

'Bertie Wiggins!' she said. 'Stop that at once. If you spent as much time on your work as you spend twitching your ears, you'd be as clever as Prince Cecil.'

Everyone in the class grinned. They all knew that Bertie looked a bit like Prince Cecil.

Bertie sighed. He was fed up with jokes about looking like a prince.

'I hope you are all going to watch Prince Cecil this evening,' said Mrs Lines.

Everyone knew how clever Prince Cecil was. Prince Cecil was very good at sums. Prince Cecil knew his tables.

Every year the King went on television and one of his children went on with him. Last year it was Princess Maude playing her trombone.

This year it was going to be Prince Cecil saying his tables.

A huge crowd went to the royal television show. Every year at the end, the crowd had to clap and cheer. Then the King made a big speech. He always began, 'Cleverness shows in many ways. It is most wonderful when it shows in someone young. The royal children…'

Every time the royal children were on television, Bertie's mum and dad would moan at Bertie. 'You may look like Prince Cecil,' they would say, 'but you'll never get on television by flapping your ears.'

That afternoon Bertie had his tea and started doing his homework. After a few minutes, he gave up and turned on the television. A lady was speaking. 'Tonight, everyone must see Prince Cecil.' Bertie turned the television off.

He went outside and sat on the
doorstep. From next door he could hear
music playing on the radio. Bertie began
to wiggle his ears. First the left one. Then
the right one. In no time at all both ears
were waggling backwards and forwards
in time to the music.

Mrs Green from next door came past.
'That's good, Bertie,' she cried. 'You're a
real little act, you are.'

'No one else seems to think so,'
grumbled Bertie.

The secret search

Just then, a car drove slowly into Bertie's street. It stopped right outside Bertie's house. A man and a woman got out. The man had a photo. To Bertie's surprise, they walked over to him.

The man looked at Bertie. Then he looked at the photo. 'It's amazing,' he said.

Bertie's mum and dad came outside. 'What's going on?' asked Mr Wiggins.

'We are from the Royal Palace,' said the woman. 'Prince Cecil has got red spots. It could be chicken pox. He can't be on the royal television show this evening. The King has ordered a secret search for a Prince Cecil look-alike.'

She pulled out a crown and put it on Bertie's head. The man held up the photo.

Mrs Wiggins gasped. 'It's our Bertie,' she cried.

'No, it's not,' said the man. 'It's Prince Cecil. We need your lad to take Prince Cecil's place on the show tonight.'

Mr Wiggins opened his mouth. Then he closed it again. At last he said, 'On television? Our Bertie? So we'll all be famous!'

'No you won't,' snapped the woman. 'No one will ever know. When Bertie goes on television this evening, everyone must think *he* is the prince. It's a secret you'll have to keep for ever.'

'Will we meet the King and Queen?' said Bertie's mum.

'Will there be a reward?' said Bertie's dad.

'Maybe,' said the man. 'But now we must get Bertie to the television studio.'

Bertie felt his blood run cold. Wasn't Prince Cecil going on television to do sums and say his tables? Bertie couldn't even get past his three times table. And as for sums... 'But Mum! But Dad!' said Bertie. It was no good. Nobody would listen.

Before Bertie could say any more, he was in the car with his mum and dad. They were on their way.

Bertie sat in the back of the car. He was very worried. How could he pretend to be Prince Cecil?

'We will go to the television studio now,' said the woman. 'Bertie has to get ready. And we must do something about his ears.'

At last Bertie gasped, 'But Prince Cecil is supposed to show how clever he is. He's supposed to say his tables. I can't do that!'

The woman sniffed. 'You don't have to be clever. All the answers will be on a screen in front of you.' She stared at him. 'You can read, can't you?'

'Of course I can,' said Bertie.

'Good,' she went on. 'No one else will be able to see the screen. No one will know that you can't do your tables.'

The King was pacing up and down in the television studio. 'I will not wait any longer!' he shouted. 'They must have found someone who looks like Cecil by now.'

At that moment, Mr and Mrs Wiggins arrived with Bertie.

Mr Wiggins bowed. 'This is Bertie,' he said. 'I'm glad we can help out, Your Majesty.'

The King looked at Bertie. He smiled. 'It's amazing,' he said. 'You could be Cecil, apart from the ears. Put Cecil's crown on and hide your ears.'

'But Your Majesty,' said Bertie. 'I am not Prince Cecil. I don't want to pretend to be him.'

'Nonsense,' said the King. 'You look like him. That's all that matters. Just do what you're told and read what's on the screen.'

It was time for the show to start. The people were in their seats. Bertie sat on a large chair. Music played. Then a man with a big smile spoke into the camera. 'Good evening, everyone. Tonight we are happy to welcome our young prince on the show. Prince Cecil is going to say his eight times table. What a clever lad!'

GOOD
EVENING
EVERYONE!
TONIGHT
WE ARE
HAPPY TO

Autocue

1

Lights shone on Bertie. A lady with headphones counted up to five on her fingers. A voice in his ear said, 'Now – ' And Bertie was on television.

Bertie felt his heart beating. He looked for the screen with the answers. There it was in front of him. He coughed, and began to read. 'One times eight is eight,' he said loudly.

Then the screen went blank.

Bertie adds it up

Bertie's tummy felt as if it had insects buzzing around inside. He wanted to be sick. He knew what came next so he gasped, 'Two times eight is sixteen.' What was three times eight?

His ears began to twitch. Prince Cecil's crown wobbled from side to side. Bertie felt the crown slip over his eyes in little jerks.

He took the crown off. This seemed to stop his ears twitching.

Then the man spoke again. He did not sound so happy now. 'Well, Prince Cecil, what are three times eight?'

Bertie tried to count the answer out on his fingers. He took off his shoes and socks and counted on his toes as well. But it was no good. He just didn't have enough fingers and toes.

One or two people called out, 'Come on! What are three times eight?' Bertie felt awful. He wanted to shout, 'I'm not Prince Cecil. I'm Bertie Wiggins.' But he couldn't say a word.

Then something strange happened. Bertie's ears began to move again. They slowly flapped back and forwards.

The crowd began to count along. 'One... two... three...' The ears flapped twenty-four times, which is exactly three times eight.

Someone shouted, 'What about four times eight?'

The ears wiggled thirty-two times.

'His ears have got it right!' cried two ladies in the front row. The crowd cheered.

By the time Bertie's ears had counted out ten times eight, the crowd were jumping up and down with excitement.

The man looked at the King. He looked at Bertie. He didn't know what to do. 'Er... Thank you, Prince Cecil... um... Or should I say, "Thanks to Prince Cecil's ears?"'

Everyone laughed, but the King scowled. 'Now the prince will do sums,' he shouted.

'Stop it, Dad!' cried a voice.

Two children darted across the studio.
One was Princess Maude. The other was
the real Prince Cecil. Now there were two
Prince Cecils in front of the camera.

Princess Maude pointed at Bertie.
'This is not Prince Cecil,' she said.

'No, I'm Bertie Wiggins,' said Bertie.

Everyone gasped. The King went red
in the face. Mrs Wiggins fainted.

Princess Maude went on, 'Prince Cecil is not very good at sums. He hates going on television. We both do. Last year I had to pretend to play the trombone. I can't really play at all.'

By now the King had jumped to his feet. He began to roar, 'Stop the show! Cecil! You should be in bed with spots. Maude! Be quiet!'

But Princess Maude took no notice. 'I painted Cecil with red spots.'

'You!' cried the King.

'Yes,' said Prince Cecil. 'But we didn't think you would find someone who looks like me.'

'So we came here by taxi,' went on Princess Maude. 'We had to stop this stupid show. We hate it because it makes everyone laugh at us. They think we're too good to be true.'

The King put his head in his hands.

'But we have always gone on the royal television show. That's what it's for.'

'Yes,' said the man. He did not look happy at all. 'What about my show?'

'I know,' said Bertie bravely. 'Why don't you put on a show that children will really like? Children from all over the country could go on it.'

'Wow! Talent spotting,' said Prince
Cecil. 'What a good idea.'

'Go on, Dad,' said Princess Maude.
'Say yes.'

The King went white and then he
went red. Then he went purple. But
everyone in the studio began to clap
and cheer.

'Well... all right,' he said. 'But my
children must tell everyone what to do.'

'No, Dad,' said Prince Cecil. 'We never want to show off again.'

'Then Bertie can do all his tables,' boomed the King. 'And he can teach everyone sums with his ears.'

Prince Cecil and Princess Maude groaned.

'No sums, thank you,' said Bertie. Then he grinned. He was enjoying himself on television. He wiggled his ears. 'But you wait. One day I'll really be the star of the show.'

About the author

I was born in London in 1963, the youngest of seven children. At least twice a day I see something worth writing about.

Once I saw an elephant pushing a shopping trolley around a supermarket car park. I really did. The poor elephant had run away from a circus. I didn't know this at the time and I thought he was looking for his car. Perhaps in a story he could have been?

In case you are wondering, Erica James is not her real name. It is a pen name for a well-known children's writer.